Rat Horoscope 2025

By

IChingHunFùyǒu FengShuisu

Table of Contents

Introduce 5

Year of the Rat (Fire) | (1948) & (2008) 8

    Overview 8

    Career and Business 10

    Financial 11

    Family 12

    Love 13

    Health 14

Year of the Rat (Earth) | (1960) & (2020) 15

    Overview 15

    Career and Business 16

    Financial 17

    Family 18

    Love 19

    Health 20

Year of the Rat (Wood) | (1972) 22

    Overview 22

    Career and Business 23

    Financial 24

    Family 25

    Love 26

    Health 27

Year of the Rat (Golden) | (1984) 28

    Overview 28

    Career and Business 29

    Financial 30

    Family 31

Love...32

Health..33

Year of the Rat (Water) | (1996) 34

Overview..34

Career and Business 35

Financial..37

Family..38

Love...39

Health..40

Chinese Astrology Horoscope for Each Month 41

Month 12 in the Dragon Year (5 Jan 25- 2 Feb 25)............................41

Month 1 in the Snake Year (3 Feb 25 - 4 Mar 25) 43

Month 2 in the Snake Year (5 Mar 25 - 3 Apr 25) 45

Month 3 in the Snake Year (4 Apr 25 - 4 May 25).............................46

Month 4 in the Snake Year (5 May 25 - 4 Jun 25) 48

Month 5 in the Snake Year (5 Jun 25 - 6 Jul 25)................................50

Month 6 in the Snake Year (7 Jul 25 - 6 Aug 25)...............................52

Month 7 in the Snake Year (7 Aug 25 - 6 Sep 25).............................54

Month 8 in the Snake Year (7 Sep 25 - 7 Oct 25)..............................56

Month 9 in the Snake Year (8 Oct 25 - 6 Nov 25).............................58

Month 10 in the Snake Year (7 Nov 25 - 6 Dec 25) 60

Month 11 in the Snake Year (7 Dec 25 - 5 Jan 25) 63

Amulet for The Year of the Rat..66

Introduce

The character of people born in the year of the rat

Rats prefer to live in packs. You have a large community as a result of your habitual politeness. There are numerous connections. On the other hand, allowing anyone to enter into a deep relationship with each other is extremely rare. You appear to be a patient individual who is unconcerned about the end of the world. But you're nervous because of the relaxed atmosphere. You value your solitude and privacy. Anyone who enters your life uninvitedly will be dizzy from your sharp lips. Rats are self-centered, stubborn creatures who prefer to solve problems on their own. Personal transactions where no one will threaten or cause problems. Parents who enjoy playing with their children are known as rat parents.

People born in this year are typically smart, intelligent, and capable of surviving. Beliefs of the ancient Chinese If there are mice in the house, it is believed that food will be plentiful throughout the year.

Strength:
Rat people have a high level of intelligence. It also conceals the habit of cheating and preferring to socialize first. People born in this year are frequently successful entrepreneurs.

Weaknesses:
 As a result of being overly ambitious, frequently leads to mistakes.

Love:
People born this year have less romantic love as a result of a mischievous child's personality. People born in this year, on the other hand, simply love someone who adores and despises someone who worships. As a result, those who want to break the heart of someone born this year should reconsider their urgent plan. People born in this year are lovely. However, the love of the year is not always long-lasting. We have a simple love habit. The habit is not

stubborn, prefers consistency, and is frequently obsessed with eroticism.

Suitable Career:

People born in the year of the rat are classified as belonging to the water element. Opening a store, selling liquor, beer, and seafood, opening a shipping company, building a boat, developing a tour company, a diplomat, an accountant, a finance company, a salesman, a broker, a negotiating job, a job related to the sale of metal and jewelry, selling jewelry or machinery, etc. are all appropriate occupations for those born in the year of the rat.

Year of the Rat (Fire) | (1948) & (2008)

"The Rat in the Barn" is a person born in the year of the Rat at the age of 77 years (1948) and 17 years (2008)

Overview

For seniors in this age group, this year is influenced by stars that cause high volatility and change. In addition to being careful about interfering in the work or personal matters of others, which will cause arguments, you must also consider your health as a top priority, both in terms of accidents and illnesses. In addition, there is another thing you should do, which is to let go of your children and grandchildren. This year, you should avoid being too naughty or involved, especially during the 3rd Chinese month (April 4 - May 4), the 5th Chinese month (June 5 - July 6), the 9th Chinese month (October 8 - November 6), and the 10th Chinese month (November 7 - December 6), which may cause emotional irritation. Turning a blind eye to things will be beneficial and bring peace to the family.

For teenagers, the planets that are moving into your horoscope this year are the Virtue and Moon planets and the Happiness and Fortune planets. This year is considered another year that will receive auspicious power to enhance your horoscope, especially in terms of education, which will have a great development in the direction of progress. There will be opportunities to study both domestically and internationally. However, because the horoscope planet "Kuo Hu" (the lawsuit planet) is moving into the horoscope, it causes your mind to be distracted by temptations around you, which may cause you to deviate. Therefore, if friends invite you to do something, you should consider choosing only things that will not cause harm to yourself and others. In addition, if you have to make contracts or do other legal transactions, this year you need to be more careful. Also, when driving on the road, you should be careful and always behave within the framework of the law so that you will not suffer from the suffering that will follow.

Career and Business

The career of both horoscopes this year is coming to a test, especially for teenagers who are studying. Although they will find auspicious stars to support them, there are also many bad stars around them. The environment tends to lead them astray, so they should be mindful and determined to study.

Group activities should be done with caution. There may be damage or loss of property, especially during the months when your work and study are likely to encounter many obstacles, such as the 3rd Chinese month (April 4 – May 4), the 5th Chinese month (June 5 – July 6), the 9th Chinese month (October 8 – November 6), and the 10th Chinese month (November 7 – December 6). Both horoscopes should avoid getting involved in matters that are not their business.

When signing or endorsing any contracts, whether for study or work, the details should be carefully checked, as they may cause problems later. The months when career and study directions will be bright and prosperous are the 12th Chinese month (January 5 – February 2), the 2nd Chinese month (March 5 – April 3), the 4th Chinese month (May 5 – June 4), and the 6th Chinese month (July 7 – August 6).

Financial

This year, your finances are in a fair range. During some periods, you may receive a large sum of money, but you cannot be greedy because money from good fortune, when it comes in, will also easily flow out. Therefore, you should know your limits and save often, especially during unfavorable months. This will cause your finances to be stuck and have problems. Be careful of unexpected expenses, such as the 3rd Chinese month (April 4 – May 4), the 5th Chinese month (June 5 – July 6), the 9th Chinese month (October 8 – November 6), and the 10th Chinese month (November 7 – December 6). You should avoid gambling and risky transactions. Do not make financial guarantees. Do not do businesses that are close to illegal matters. Do not be greedy for fortunes that do not belong to you. It will bring disaster to you. The months when your finances will flow smoothly are the 12th Chinese month (January 5 – February 2), the 2nd Chinese month (March 5 – April 3), the 4th Chinese month (May 5 – June 4), and the 6th Chinese month (July 7 – August 6).

Family

This year, family horoscopes should be careful about arguments, especially with neighbors. Therefore, you should be patient and compromise, and always strengthen and maintain good relationships to rely on each other when there is danger from others. This year, both horoscopes of both age groups must be careful of losing belongings from juniors or thieves. Therefore, valuables should be kept hidden, especially in the following months when you should be more careful about unexpected events: the 3rd Chinese month (April 4 - May 4), the 5th Chinese month (June 5 - July 6), the 9th Chinese month 9 (October 8 - November 6), and 10th Chinese month (November 7 - December 6). In addition, during these months, seniors should be careful of arguments with people in the house. Some things may seem unpleasant, but you should let it go. You can find time to go to the temple to pay respect to the deities, which will help you feel calm and relaxed. For teenagers during this period, when joining a group to hang out, you should consider the place you go because there may be dangers.

Love

For the elderly, the truth of this age requires love and attention from children and grandchildren. However, since each person has overwhelming responsibilities, the relationship may seem rather distant and indifferent. They may not be able to take care of you at times. You may have to accept it. Acting like a warm and friendly advisor is better than criticizing and nagging you to do as you wish. In some matters, you may have to close your eyes and not get involved too much. You will receive love from those close to you as usual.

For the young generation, love this year may not go as you wish. However, before accusing the other person, please consider your behavior. The months in which your love will easily have problems and arguments are the 3rd Chinese month (April 4 – May 4), the 5th Chinese month (June 5 – July 6), the 9th Chinese month (October 8 – November 6), and the 10th Chinese month (November 7 – December 6).

Health

The health of both horoscopes this year is not good because the evil stars "Pae Hu" (star of illness) and "Keng Hu" (star of sickness) are disturbing the horoscope houses. Therefore, the months when you need to be careful and take care of your health closely are the 3rd Chinese month (April 4 – May 4), the 5th Chinese month (June 5 – July 6), the 9th Chinese month (October 8 – November 6), and the 10th Chinese month (November 7 – December 6). For the elderly, you need to control your weight and pay attention to your diet. Limit sweet, fatty, salty, and hard-to-digest foods. You should also be careful of slipping and falling. For teenagers, you should be careful of car accidents and be careful of fights at gatherings.

While you are out, you are likely to get caught in the crossfire or pick a fight with others.

Year of the Rat (Earth) | (1960) & (2020)

"The Rat in the beam" is a person born in the year of the Rat at the age of 65 years (1960) and 5 years (2020)

Overview

For those with a 65-year-old horoscope, this year is considered a passable year. However, you should not be careless. All work activities should be reviewed before starting, especially large investments. You cannot be hasty. In terms of work or business, this year you will be affected by unexpected external changes and problems and obstacles will appear at the same time. However, luckily, your horoscope will receive help from the auspicious stars, which will help turn some crises into opportunities and lighten the burden.

For children with a 5-year-old horoscope, this year your studies will go well and you will see progress. However, because of the negative energy from the enemy stars, your child will be quite naughty and hyperactive. Parents should therefore take care of them closely to prevent accidents.

Career and Business

This year, your career is quite volatile. In terms of management, you should have a backup plan to prepare for situations that may change. You should also look for an heir or assistant to succeed you. This will help things flow smoothly from a different perspective and will not make you too tired in a constantly changing situation. The months when your work will be hindered and have obstacles and problems are the 3rd Chinese month (April 4 - May 4), the 5th Chinese month (June 5 - July 6), the 9th Chinese month (October 8 - November 6), and the 10th Chinese month (November 7 - December 6). During this period, do not let your emotions get the better of you because you will need to cooperate with others for the work to be successful. You should be extra careful when signing documents and contracts, and be careful of hidden tricks.

In addition, you should not interfere with other people's work. This year, your work horoscope will be bright. There will be opportunities for joint investment or joint ventures to do business, which will have a good response, especially in the months when your work will change in a good direction. Including the smooth trading of the following months: the 12th Chinese month (January 5 – February 2), the 2nd Chinese month (March 5 – April 3), the 4th Chinese month (May 5 – June 4), and the 6th Chinese month (July 7 – August 6).

Financial

This year, your finances are in a bad state. Investing a large sum of money still has risks. There is a high possibility of being affected by external economic fluctuations or unpredictable events. Therefore, you should plan your finances carefully and save up emergency funds to help you survive the crisis. However, it would be better to tighten your belt if you can save money, especially during the months when your finances will be interrupted and have problems, such as the 3rd Chinese month (April 4 - May 4), the 5th Chinese month (June 5 - July 6), the 9th Chinese month (October 8 - November 6), and the 10th Chinese month (November 7 - December 6). You should not lend money to others. Avoid doing big business, including investing in a trade that is likely to be illegal. Do not sign financial guarantees. Do not be greedy for wealth that does not belong to you. Be careful that your account will have mistakes that will expose the truth, whether due to carelessness or some things that indicate fraud. The months when your finances will flow smoothly are the 12th Chinese month (January 5 – February 2), the 2nd Chinese month (March 5 – April 3), the 4th Chinese month (May 5 – June 4), and the 6th Chinese month (July 7 – August 6).

Family

This year, the family horoscope is moderate. There are things to be careful about accidents in the home or unexpected events that cause family members to suffer from bloodshed.

However, if this year your family has the opportunity to organize an auspicious event, it will help reduce the disaster. The months in which your family will experience problems and conflicts are the 3rd Chinese month (April 4 - May 4), the 5th Chinese month (June 5 - July 6), the 9th Chinese month (October 8 - November 6), and the 10th Chinese month (November 7 - December 6). During these periods, be careful of valuables in the home that may be lost or stolen. Be careful of arguments or accidents among family members.

In addition, be careful of being too considerate of yourself, as you will be disturbed more by others. Also, do not reveal everything you say because it will be a danger to yourself. For children, this year, parents should not leave their children alone. Be careful of strangers who will come to deceive you.

Love

This year's love horoscope is considered to be full of ups and downs. For those who have been married for a long time, being angry and not giving in to the other person is like a cloud covering the sky. When the sunlight shines, the black clouds move away and the sky instantly becomes bright again. The months when your love life will easily experience problems and resentment are the 3rd Chinese month (April 4 - May 4), the 5th Chinese month (June 5 - July 6), the 9th Chinese month (October 8 - November 6), and the 10th Chinese month (November 7 - December 6). Be careful of arguing. You should not meddle in other people's family matters. Be careful that your kindness will make younger people want to get close to you, but it will cause bigger problems later. During months that are not supportive, you should avoid going to entertainment venues. It will cause endless trouble.

Health

This year, the health of the elderly is not very good. You should be careful of old diseases recurring, liver disease, high blood pressure, and latent diseases that may occur to internal organs, especially in the following months when you should pay close attention to your health: the 3rd Chinese month (April 4 - May 4), 5th Chinese month (June 5 - July 6), 9th Chinese month (October 8 - November 6), and the 10th Chinese month (November 7 - December 6). The elderly should observe their bodies and go for regular health check-ups. Be strict with yourself about what you eat and drink, and take your medicine as prescribed by the doctor strictly.

In addition, safety must be the number one priority when using the road. As for the health of the young children this year, it is not good or bad. Be careful of dangers in the water. When traveling long distances or going to strange places, there should be adults to closely supervise.

Year of the Rat (Wood) | (1972)

" The Rat on the Mountain" is a person born in the year of the Rat at the age of 53 years (1972)

Overview

For the Rat horoscope in this age group, this year, whether it is about work or business, there will be a good direction of prosperity and progress. Various investments are likely to have good numbers and profits. Therefore, it is a good opportunity to expand work and investment or increase production. You will have the opportunity to buy expensive assets or organize auspicious events.

However, during the year, four bad stars will appear, which will cause bad results and disasters at certain times, especially affecting the safety of family members. Be careful of health problems and accidents. Therefore, if you have time, you should check the safety of your belongings, fixtures, electrical equipment, and others. Also, be careful of arguments that sometimes small things can become big things. There will be long-term lawsuits. Therefore, this year, some things that are dissatisfied must be postponed. You cannot let your emotions take over. Reconciliation is better than disputes. When the house is peaceful, money will come to you. Your work will be smooth and your life will be happy.

Career and Business

Your business this year is considered to be prosperous and bright, a sign of progress. Therefore, if you are more diligent and plan in the right direction, it will mean more financial income. Therefore, you should not let time pass without creating benefits. However, you should be careful of the months when your work will encounter problems and difficulties, which are the 3rd Chinese month (April 4 - May 4), the 5th Chinese month (June 5 - July 6), the 9th Chinese month (October 8 - November 6), and the 10th Chinese month (November 7 - December 6). When signing an employment contract or being hired for work, be careful of being deceived or there may be ambiguous terms in the contract that will put you at a disadvantage in the future. Be careful of subordinates or subordinates causing trouble. Avoid investing during this period, which is very risky. Be careful of capital stumbling from external conditions that are beyond expectations. Be careful of errors in the accounting system, both from carelessness and internal corruption.

In addition, be careful of being deceived in various forms by using returns to lure you. For the months when your work and business will have a change in a bright direction, they are the 12th Chinese month (January 5 – February 2), the 2nd Chinese month (March 5 – April 3), the 4th Chinese month (May 5 – June 4), and the 6th Chinese month (July 7 – August 6).

Financial

This year, your finances are in good shape. Both direct income from sales or salary, as well as money from windfalls, are all possible. In addition, business investment, buying bonds, bills of exchange, or buying gold are all in a bright direction. However, you should be careful during the months when your finances will be tight and unexpected expenses will occur, which are the 3rd Chinese month (April 4 – May 4), the 5th Chinese month (June 5 – July 6), the 9th Chinese month (October 8 – November 6), and the 10th Chinese month (November 7 – December 6). Do not lend money to others. Do not sign as a guarantor for others. Avoid gambling and taking risks in various aspects. Also, do not do immoral or illegal businesses. Do not be greedy for wealth that does not belong to you. The months when your finances will flow smoothly are the 12th Chinese month (January 5 – February 2), the 2nd Chinese month (March 5 – April 3), the 4th Chinese month (May 5 – June 4), and the 6th Chinese month (July 7 – August 6).

Family

This year's family horoscope, since the Tiang Hee star (Fa Yindee) is located in the horoscope house, you will likely move to a new place of work, buy expensive property, have an auspicious event in your home, or you may have a new family member. However, you should be careful during the months when your family will have conflicts, which are the 3rd Chinese month (April 4 – May 4), the 5th Chinese month (June 5 – July 6), the 9th Chinese month (October 8 – November 6), and the 10th Chinese month (November 7 – December 6). You should be careful of valuables in your home being damaged or lost due to thieves. Be careful of accidents that may happen to people in your home. Be careful of arguing over small matters that may lead to disputes that may turn into lawsuits. In addition, you should not get involved in other people's conflicts. Also, be careful of some friends who pretend to be innocent but have ulterior motives.

Love

This year is another year where your love life is quite sweet. You will have the opportunity to take your lover or spouse on a long trip

make merit together in the provinces or abroad or organize charity events to help those affected by natural disasters or the poor in remote areas. However, there are some periods of the year when your love will be fragile and easily cause arguments, including:

The 3rd Chinese month (April 4 – May 4), the 5th Chinese month (June 5 – July 6), the 9th Chinese month (October 8 – November 6) and the 10th Chinese month (November 7 – December 6). Do not interfere in other people's family matters. Avoid going to entertainment venues that sell services. In addition, you should have a strong mind. Do not be easily influenced by words of incitement to harm.

Health

Your health this year is moderate. You should be careful of health problems related to heart disease, stress accumulation that causes insomnia, and eating indulgently that causes various diseases such as high blood pressure, high cholesterol, gout, and food poisoning. The months when you should pay close attention to your health and take care of yourself are the 3rd Chinese month (April 4 – May 4), the 5th Chinese month (June 5 – July 6), the 9th Chinese month (October 8 – November 6), and the 10th Chinese month (November 7 – December 6). You should get enough rest, observe your symptoms, and get a health check-up before your illness flares up. Don't be careless when traveling near or far and on the road.

Year of the Rat (Golden) | (1984)

" The Rat in the House" is a person born in the year of the Rat at the age of 41 years (1984)

Overview

This year in the Rat year, you will find someone to help you, making many things that are stuck smoother. This year is a year of good opportunities. Therefore, you should be diligent in your career, keep yourself updated with the current situation, and know how to approach opportunities. When you see an opportunity, don't let it pass you by. Because when you have someone to help you think and do, it's like a tiger with wings. Your work will be multiplied. When businesses receive support, sales will expand, which means more money as income. Even though during the year, there will be bad stars moving into your horoscope house.

But because you are influenced by auspicious stars, heavy bad luck will become light. The most important thing you should do this year is to develop yourself for the advancement of your life and the prosperity of your business. You shouldn't worry too much. When the opportunity opens, you have to move forward quickly. However, this year, there is something you should be careful about investing in shares or investing in stocks. In large joint ventures, you must consider your ability to continuously invest. You should also consider other conditions, from the investors and the minor contracts. Otherwise, it may cause damage later.

Career and Business

Although the overall career of the person this year is good, because the career base is being targeted by the evil star "Chi Puay" (backstabbing star), during the year, the person should be careful of some close people or subordinates who will cause trouble. All work activities should not be rushed and make decisions without thinking, especially during the bad months when your work will be stuck and easily encounter problems, namely the 3rd Chinese month (April 4 - May 4), the 5th Chinese month (June 5 - July 6), the 9th Chinese month (October 8 - November 6), and the 10th Chinese month (November 7 - December 6). When signing an employment contract or being hired, you should carefully consider the details of the contract. Be careful of careless words or actions or those caused by trust that will cause important information to be leaked. Investing during this period is very risky. Be careful of subordinates causing damage.

The months in which your career will be bright and prosperous are the 12th Chinese month (5 January – 2 February), the 2nd Chinese month (5 March – 3 April), the 4th Chinese month (5 May – 4 June), and the 6th Chinese month (7 July – 6 August).

Financial

This year, your finances will be bright with good income from direct income from salary, sales, special money from special jobs, bonuses, brokerage fees, and windfalls. As for various investments, this year's overall picture is quite smooth. It is expected that dividends and returns will be satisfactory, especially during the months when your finances will flow smoothly, which are the 12th Chinese month (January 5 – February 2), the 2nd Chinese month (March 5 – April 3), the 4th Chinese month (May 5 – June 4), and the 6th Chinese month (July 7 – August 6). As for the months when your finances will face problems and you should be careful of unexpected expenses, they are the 3rd Chinese month (April 4 – May 4), the 5th Chinese month (June 5 – July 6), the 9th Chinese month (October 8 – November 6), and the 10th Chinese month (November 7 – December 6), during which you are prohibited from lending money to others or signing guarantees to help others. Do not gamble or take risks, and do not be greedy for wealth that does not belong to you.

Family

The family picture of this age group is good. This year, you are likely to move into a new house. This is a good time to buy expensive property that you like. However, you will be annoyed with juniors who will cause trouble from time to time, from damaging things to snatching valuables and becoming mentally ill. Another important thing is to take care of the health of the elders in the house closely. The months in which your family will experience chaos are the 3rd Chinese month (April 4 – May 4), the 5th Chinese month (June 5 – July 6), the 9th Chinese month (October 8 – November 6), and the 10th Chinese month (November 7 – December 6).

Love

This year, the love aspect of the person is not so good because there are hazardous planets and the Peach Blossom Evil star in focus. Therefore, you should be mindful and calm. Do not listen to gossip and slander. Listening to only one side of the story and jumping to conclusions will easily lead to a breakup. You should also be careful about a third person who will come to test your love. You should be firm and control your behavior.

The months when you should be especially careful about love problems are the 3rd Chinese month (April 4 - May 4), the 5th Chinese month (June 5 - July 6), the 9th Chinese month (October 8 - November 6), and the 10th Chinese month (November 7 - December 6). In addition, during these months, you should not go to places of entertainment or services because you may accidentally catch an illness. Be careful of arguments with your lover or partner. Do not interfere in other people's family matters.

Health

Your overall health this year is good. You may have to spend money on minor illnesses during the year. However, you should find free time to exercise regularly. This will help relieve back pain, neck pain, and joint pain. However, you should be careful during the following months when you need to take care of your health closely: the 3rd Chinese month (April 4 - May 4), the 5th Chinese month (June 5 - July 6), the 9th Chinese month (October 8 - November 6), and the 10th Chinese month (November 7 -

December 6). Be careful of accidents while traveling, especially after a party. If you have been drinking, you should not force yourself to drive. It will be dangerous for yourself and other road users.

Year of the Rat (Water) | (1996)

" The Rat in the Field" is a person born in the year of the Rat at the age of 29 years (1996)

Overview

For the Rat horoscope in this age, in the positive aspect, this year you will receive the auspicious power of progress, so it is another good time to pioneer your life to move forward. Therefore, please devote your intelligence and abilities and increase your diligence, diligently add more skills to yourself. In your work, you will be able to create work that impresses your elders and receive support. As for those who do business, you must be diligent in making sales, analyze statistics, and visit customers often. However, in the horoscope house, there are bad stars "Chi Puay" (backstabbing star) and "Kua Hu" (litigation star) orbiting to harass and disturb, which will result in mistakes being made easily during work. In doing business, there will be problems with communication. You should also be careful of trading that violates rights, which will result in lawsuits and have to go to court. Some cases that are against the law are classified as criminal offenses that may result in imprisonment. Therefore, all activities and trades this year should be done within the framework of the law so that you will not suffer. When driving, including using vehicles on the road, do not be careless or overlook safety.

Career and Business

This year your career will be prosperous and you will find supporters. Therefore, in carrying out various work activities, you should devote yourself diligently and with determination because no matter what, your work will not disappear anywhere. You will catch the eye of your boss. This year, there will be a good time to promote you to a raise or promotion. For those who do their own business or do business, this year there will be a path of progress and you will find supporters. Businesses will expand, especially during the months when your work progresses. And business will be smooth and prosperous in the following months: the 12th Chinese month (January. 5 – February. 2), the 2nd Chinese month (March 5 – April. 3), the 4th Chinese month (May 5 – June. 4), and the 6th Chinese month (July 7 – August. 6). However, be careful in the following months when work and further education will be hindered and have problems: the 3rd Chinese month (April 4 – May 4), the 5th Chinese month (June 5 – July. 6), the 9th Chinese month (October 8 – November. 6), and the 10th Chinese month (November 7 – December. 6). When signing a contract to accept work or employment, or requesting a scholarship to continue studying with conditions on repaying the scholarship, the obligations should be carefully considered.

Financial

The finances of the Rat people in this age group are bright. Cash flows in from two sources: direct salary or sales, special money from special jobs, brokerage fees, bonuses, and windfalls. The months when the finances of the Rat people will flow smoothly are the 12th Chinese month (January 5 - February 2), the 2nd Chinese month (March 5 - April 3), the 4th Chinese month (May 5 - June 4), and the 6th Chinese month (July 7 - August 6). As for gambling, since there will be both wins and losses, you should play mindfully and not be greedy, especially during the months when the financial stars are low. You should also be careful of unexpected expenses during the 3rd Chinese month (April 4 - May 4), the 5th Chinese month (June 5 - July 6), the 9th Chinese month (October 8 - November 6), and the 10th Chinese month (November 7 - December 6). During these periods, you should not gamble, sign financial guarantees, invest in risky businesses, or participate in illegal businesses.

Family

This year, the family horoscope is bright and you will find a sponsor. The overall picture is quite good. Whatever you think will be supported by your relatives. The person will likely buy expensive property, move into a new house or workplace, and have an auspicious time to organize auspicious events. There will also be an opportunity to add new family members. However, during the year, two bad stars will appear to disturb the family: the backstabbing star and the lawsuit star, which will affect the safety of family members. There will be arguments, quarrels, and chaos both inside and outside the family, especially in the following months: the 3rd Chinese month (April 4 - May 4), the 5th Chinese month (June 5 - July 6), the 9th Chinese month (October 8 - November 6), and the 10th Chinese month (November 7 - December 6), when you need to be more careful and cautious about accidents in the home. Be careful of online threats, and valuables being damaged, lost, or stolen. Be careful of arguments and quarrels that turn small matters into big ones that will cause more damage than before.

Love

This year, your love life will be smooth and bright. Those who are single will be especially charming. The opposite sex will be interested. Those who have a partner will be well taken care of and may have good news about having a new little child as a new member of the family. It is also a good time for singles to get engaged, get married, or move out. However, some couples may encounter a third-party interfering, especially during the months when your love life will be fragile and easily prone to problems, such as the 3rd Chinese month (April 4 – May 4), the 5th Chinese month (June 5 – July 6), the 9th Chinese month (October 8 – November 6), and the 10th Chinese month (November 7 – December 6). Be careful not to get involved with other people's lovers or families. Do not go to entertainment venues that provide hidden sexual services. Be careful about arguments and illnesses that may follow.

Health

This year, your health is considered moderate, but what you should not be careless about is accidents and illnesses that require hospitalization. Therefore, while working and traveling, you should be careful to be safe. The months when you should be more careful about accidents and pay close attention to your health are the 3rd Chinese month (April 4 - May 4), the 5th Chinese month (June 5 - July 6), the 9th Chinese month (October 8 - November 6), and the 10th Chinese month (November 7 - December 6). If you attend a party, always remember not to drink and drive. If you work with machinery or have to deal with sharp tools or equipment, you should be more careful because it may be dangerous. In addition, you should arrange for enough rest and sleep so that you will be cheerful and have the energy to pioneer your work for progress.

Chinese Astrology Horoscope for Each Month

Month 12 in the Dragon Year (5 Jan 25- 2 Feb 25)
This month, the horoscope of those born in the year of the Rat is smooth and bright because it meets the month of the Ox, which is compatible. Therefore, the cash flow is still good. In addition, it is the first month of the Chinese New Year, which is considered a beautiful starting point for planning various projects to move forward. Therefore, what you should do during this period is to plan your work, set clear directions and goals, allocate investment budgets, and estimate manpower, capital, and plans. Or you can dust off old projects that you had previously planned and rework them. This is considered a green light, but you should hurry to push them into shape as soon as possible within this month. Because if it drags on until next month, there will be obstacles and problems.

This period of work is considered a bright period, suitable for investment, increasing production, expanding sales, and creating more work because you will see good returns. Therefore, you should not let this good month pass by in vain. Instead, you should be diligent and work hard. The more you do, the more you will receive.

In terms of finances, this year, if you work hard, you will receive unexpected income. The family will be peaceful. During this period, you are likely to buy expensive property into the house or some people may have the opportunity to move into a new house.

In terms of health, your body is strong and healthy. For those who have old chronic diseases that cannot be cured, this month you will meet a good doctor with good medicine to help solve the problem.

In terms of love, it is sweet. Your lover will take care of you closely and never leave you. As for close relatives and friends, this period is clear. If there are any problems, you will receive help, but you cannot expect money.

Support Days: 3 Jan., 7 Jan., 11 Jan., 15 Jan., 19 Jan., 23 Jan., 27 Jan., 31 Jan.
Lucky Days: 8 Jan., 20 Jan
Misfortune Days: 1 Jan., 13 Jan., 25 Jan
Bad Days: 2 Jan, 4 Jan, 14 Jan, 16 Jan, 26 Jan, 28 Jan.

Month 1 in the Snake Year (3 Feb 25 - 4 Mar 25)

This month, the Rat year is entering a situation that is not yet fully favorable. Although sometimes there are opportunities, you cannot be impatient in many activities. You still need to analyze and consider the situation clearly before moving forward. What you should do this month is to plug any problems that have been. Find new ways or methods. Always be prepared and be extra careful in everything.

In terms of work and trade, even though there are obstacles during this period if you use your skills in building relationships and building friendships with those you have to deal with consistently, it will help to resolve and pave the way for convenience. Especially those who have regular jobs should be kind to both their superiors and colleagues to reduce problems from work that may arise and have a smooth future.

As for joint ventures and investments in various fields, this month is quite good, but you must have enough information. Your financial luck this month is moderate. At the beginning of the year like this, there are still many expenses waiting. Therefore, you should save and be frugal in all activities. Do not lend money to others or guarantee for anyone.

In terms of family, there is peace. In terms of love, there is a chance that you will travel to do merit-making activities together. Relatives and friends will receive support if they encounter any problems.

Support Days: 4 Feb., 8 Feb., 12 Feb., 16 Feb., 20 Feb., 24 Feb., 28 Feb.
Lucky Days: 1 Feb., 13 Feb., 25 Feb.
Misfortune Days: 6 Feb., 18 Feb.
Bad Days: 7 Feb., 9 Feb., 19 Feb., 21 Feb.

Month 2 in the Snake Year (5 Mar 25 - 3 Apr 25)
This month, the life path of those born in the year of the Rat will show auspicious stars shining and driving out inauspicious energy from the horoscope house. What you should do this month is start new projects, launch new products, buy gold, or invest in something you have studied for a while. When you do and push your work until it becomes tangible, it will help many things during this period change in a good direction, and you will see clearer growth and progress.

In terms of work or business, during this period, you will find a patron to support you. Be diligent and determined, and you will be able to create beautiful results and sales.

In terms of luck, your salary will be good, but if you know how to save, it will be better than letting time pass without saving because no one will have a fixed and consistent income. Therefore, you should not be careless. You should keep a record of your income and expenses and plan your spending well.

For your family horoscope, this month, you will still love and be happy. This is another period when you are likely to buy expensive property.

As for love, this month, it is still bright, with regular visits. The relationship is still happy. As for relatives and friends, it is moderate, and you can rely on them, but not too much.

Support Days: 4 Mar., 8 Mar., 12 Mar., 16 Mar., 20 Mar., 24 Mar., 28 Mar.
Lucky Days: 9 Mar., 21 Mar.
Misfortune Days: 2 Mar., 14 Mar., 26 Mar.
Bad Days: 3 Mar., 5 Mar., 15 Mar., 17 Mar., 27 Mar., 29 Mar.

Month 3 in the Snake Year (4 Apr 25 - 4 May 25)
This month, your fate will fall dramatically. Your career and business will face high pressure from many problems that have accumulated, both old and new. Various operations are not as smooth as you would like. Therefore, what you should do during this period is to concentrate and prepare to deal

with obstacles. Do not interfere or interfere with the responsibilities of others. When work comes in, you should hurry to finish it.

Do not leave it hanging, it will only make things more complicated. Because during this period, your career and business will often face events or problems that challenge your abilities. You will need to be mindful and calm to cope with it, so you will be able to overcome the crisis. Investments are not good. You still have to sing and wait for a while.

This month, your financial luck will be normal in terms of sales and regular income, but if you expect to gain from gambling, you should be careful. It is better not to gamble, it is safer.

In terms of family, be careful during this period because there will be a problem that will cost you money for the medical expenses of people in the house. You will also have to take responsibility for the misfortunes caused by subordinates or subordinates.

In terms of love, life will be normal.

As for your health, you will get a little sick. However, both during work and travel, be careful of accidents, especially with close friends and relatives. During this time, stay away from friends who like to invite you to go out because accidents may occur while traveling.

Support Days: 1 Apr., 5 Apr., 9 Apr., 13 Apr., 17 Apr., 21 Apr., 25 Apr., 29 Apr.
Lucky Days: 2 Apr., 14 Apr., 26 Apr.
Misfortune Days: 7 Apr., 19 Apr.
Bad Days: 8 Apr., 10 Apr., 20 Apr., 22Apr.

Month 4 in the Snake Year (5 May 25 - 4 Jun 25)
This month, the horoscope of those born in the year of the Rat will return to good, resulting in work that will find a path of progress. Business will flourish. Therefore, what you should do on this occasion is to prepare all the factors for more work.

Increase sales and income under a peaceful situation. Strike while the fire is hot. Hold on to the timing and opportunities that come your way. Look for something different and expand the results to flourish. As for joint ventures and starting a new job, opportunities are open for this period. Investing in various areas during this period will have satisfactory returns. This month's financial horoscope is good, with abundant income flowing in. There is also a chance of receiving a windfall from taking risks in various areas. However, if you win and don't stop, you have a chance to withdraw it.

Family horoscope is good, you will receive good news or have the opportunity to organize an auspicious event in the house.

In terms of love, this is a sweet time, suitable for couples to take time to review and return to love by going on a honeymoon for the second or third time. Singles will be charming and have the opposite sex flocking to love them. For those with love problems, this is a good time to adjust and understand each other.

In terms of health, please take good care of yourself during this period to support your work. Beware of food poisoning, diarrhea, and loose stools. If your relatives or friends are in trouble, they will still receive help and support.

Support Days: 3 May., 7 May., 11 May., 15 May., 19 May., 23 May., 27 May., 31 May.
Lucky Days: 8 May., 20 May.
Misfortune Days: 1 May., 13 May., 25 May.
Bad Days: 2 May., 4 May., 14 May., 16 May., 26 May., 28 May.

Month 5 in the Snake Year (5 Jun 25 - 6 Jul 25)
This month, the horoscope of those born in the year of the Rat has moved into the "Bo-Ngow" energy line, causing the horoscope to be shaken and shaken, affecting safety and being easily affected by unexpected external events. What you should do this month is that every step you take must not be based on carelessness. You should also use your mindfulness to control your emotions and not offend others because you lack self-control. Also, during this period, be careful that your love life will fall into a crisis, which may be caused by a love disease

because you went to an entertainment venue without protection.

This month, your finances will be spent on the left and the right. Your money will be spinning like a spiral. Avoid investing in large sums of money and you should not gamble. Do not do business related to copyright infringement, immorality, or illegal activities because the star of lawsuits, "Kuo-Hu", is still shining and trying to harm you during this period.

In terms of work, you will encounter the same old problems repeatedly. You may need to use more decisive measures and find a way to deal with them nicely, otherwise, you will encounter the same problems again and again. In this period, family events are another month where you need to be careful about accidents and take care of the health of your family members.

For love, do not let carelessness, and temporary happiness, turn into long-term suffering. This month, all things related to relatives, investing, starting a new job, and investing are not good.

Support Days: 4 Jun., 8 Jun., 12 Jun., 16 Jun., 20 Jun., 24 Jun., 28 Jun.
Lucky Days: 1 Jun., 13 Jun., 25 Jun.
Misfortune Days: 6 Jun., 18 Jun., 30 Jun.
Bad Days: 7 Jun., 9 Jun., 19 Jun., 21 Jun.

Month 6 in the Snake Year (7 Jul 25 - 6 Aug 25)

This month, the horoscope of those born in the year of the Rat is considered to have passed the clashing power. Many events around you are gradually turning around and becoming bright. Some things that seemed to be going nowhere are starting to get better. Work and businesses that are stuck will encounter obstacles. There will be a patron to help. Therefore, during this month, you should not be discouraged and slow down. Instead, you should focus on finding new knowledge to get back to work. Even though there is still dark energy left, you should not be discouraged or let time go to waste. The important thing you should do during this time is to use past mistakes as a lesson. Learn more about new technologies to save energy and time. You must also maintain relationships with those you have to contact to deepen your friendship beyond just sellers and customers, including those you have to contact. This will allow you to have many people help you in the future.

This month's financial criteria is moderate income. The important thing during this period is that you should not be too blinded by the benefits that others bring to tempt you. You will easily fall into the trap of scammers. Remember that no one will give you anything for free.

Family is peaceful. Love is also a calm period. However, you must be strong-willed. Don't be swayed by the other person's provocative words and your love life will be happy.

Health is moderate. Be careful of accidents during work and travel. Relatives can still be a source of support. However, investing, starting a new job, and investing in various things are not good opportunities.

Support Days: 2 Jul., 6 Jul., 10 Jul., 14 Jul., 18 Jul., 22 Jul., 26 Jul., 30 Jul.
Lucky Days: 7 Jul., 19 Jul., 31 Jul.
Misfortune Days: 12 Jul., 24 Jul.
Bad Days: 1 Jul., 3 Jul., 13 Jul., 15 Jul., 25 Jul., 27 Jul.

Month 7 in the Snake Year (7 Aug 25 - 6 Sep 25)
This month is a month for Rat people because the power of conflict is still spreading. Many things that seem to be going on normally are still hidden with problems. Therefore, you cannot be confident in the situation. Therefore, what you should do this month that will help you stay safe is to avoid getting involved in other people's matters. Always build good relationships with people you have to contact, both old and new, consistently. Do not act arrogantly or show off your skills. It will be dangerous. Be kind and generous and do good things for those close to you. Then you will receive kindness and help to solve many problems and survive the crisis.

This month's financial horoscope is normal. You cannot expect a windfall and be careful of liquidity shortages. Therefore, do not lend money to others or accept guarantees. Do not do business that is likely to be illegal. Also, you should refrain from spending money extravagantly because it will not only waste your money but also your health.

In terms of work, there will be changes for the better. You still need to keep adding knowledge and learn to adjust to things around you. Your family will be peaceful.

Entering into a partnership or starting a new job this month is considered good. It is a period of opportunity. Both internal and external investments are expected to return according to plan.

In terms of love, this period has auspicious times for asking for love, getting engaged, and getting married.

Your health is good. However, you should exercise and eat healthy food to be on the safe side.

Support Days: 3 Aug., 7 Aug., 11 Aug., 15 Aug., 19 Aug., 23 Aug., 27 Aug., 31 Aug.
Lucky Days: 12 Aug., 24 Aug.
Misfortune Days: 5 Aug., 17 Aug., 29 Aug.
Bad Days: 6 Aug., 8 Aug., 18 Aug., 20 Aug., 30 Aug.

Month 8 in the Snake Year (7 Sep 25 - 7 Oct 25)
This month is neither good nor bad. You cannot reduce your diligence. And there is something you should be careful of jealousy from people close to you will turn into evil. Therefore, the most important thing you should do during this period is to be fair. If you are a boss or doing business, dividing the appropriate portion will gain trust and faith. Everyone will reciprocate the kindness of each other. If you are a worker, do not be selfish to the point that your friends or colleagues feel taken advantage of. It will only create a waste of yourself.

In terms of work or business during this period, even though there are some problems, if you are sincere in trying to understand each other, it will help turn bad things into good things.

In terms of luck and finance, this period is on the rise. Picking up or planning any project is unlikely to fail. There will be a return in the form of a beautiful number in the account. However, you should not expect too much windfall profit. Focus on direct profit, which will be more visible.

Within your family during this period, there will be unrest. There will often be arguments and disagreements among family members. Also, be careful of subordinates or servants in the house having problems with neighbors, which will cause trouble.

In terms of love, it is still smooth and normal. You will have the opportunity to travel or go on a long trip to visit relatives together.

For good health, friends will provide warm care and advice, and help solve critical problems. For starting a new job or investing in various channels, it is still a good direction.

Support Days: 4 Sep., 8 Sep., 12 Sep., 16 Sep., 20 Sep., 24 Sep., 28 Sep., 29 Sep.
Lucky Days: 5 Sep., 17 Sep., 29 Sep.
Misfortune Days: 10 Sep., 22 Sep.
Bad Days: 1 Sep., 11 Sep., 13 Sep., 23 Sep., 25 Sep.

Month 9 in the Snake Year (8 Oct 25 - 6 Nov 25)
Entering this month, the evil star "Kuo Hu" (the star of lawsuits) is moving in to disturb and threaten, causing your horoscope to fall out of its orbit. Things you expected and intended to do have started to break ranks, cheat, and not go according to plan, and many unexpected things have appeared. Therefore, during this period, what you should do is to be mindful that every activity requires patience and endurance to get through the crisis.

This month's financial luck is also not encouraging. Be careful that during some periods, large expenses will interfere, which may cause you to lack liquidity. In addition, be careful of accounting errors, seeing hidden details or some of you may have problems with the Revenue Department. Also, during this period, you should not be greedy and hope for other people's wealth or money. Be careful that you will lose your own money instead.

In terms of work and trade, during this period, obstacles and problems will come crashing down. Be careful that subordinates will bring you troubles to be responsible for. Be careful that people close to you will betray you and cause you grief.
As for starting a new job, or investing in stocks or shares, you should wait for now.

In terms of family, you should be careful of people in the house or servants who cause problems and cause loss of property. In terms of relatives, you should not interfere in other people's matters. This will only create problems in return.

In terms of love, during this time, your parents are easily quarreling and clashing with each other. You should be flexible, lenient, and patient.

In terms of health, be careful of injuries from accidents.

Support Days: 2 Oct., 6 Oct., 10 Oct., 14 Oct., 18 Oct., 22 Oct., 26 Oct., 30 Oct.
Lucky Days: 11 Oct., 23 Oct.
Misfortune Days: 4 Oct., 16 Oct., 28 Oct.
Bad Days: 5 Oct., 7 Oct., 17 Oct., 19 Oct., 29 Oct., 31 Oct.

Month 10 in the Snake Year (7 Nov 25 - 6 Dec 25)
This month, the horoscope of those born in the year of the Rat has moved to meet several bad stars that are grouped and focused, starting from the "Kuo Hu" (litigation star) and the

"Huang Pui" (reverse star) which have an influence that must be especially careful about, which is accidents, arguments, disputes, and court cases. Therefore, what you should do during this time is to build and maintain good relationships with people around you at all times. When encountering various events, you must be patient and cannot take responsibility for everything, especially matters that are not your business. Otherwise, you may suffer bad luck or good fortune later.

This month, be careful of unexpected large expenses that may drain the capital in the system, which may cause a lack of liquidity. Therefore, you should be frugal, save money, not be extravagant, and plan your finances carefully so that in times of emergency, you will not be in trouble.

In terms of work and business, during this time, be careful of being disrespectful or disrespectful, which will cause obstacles and hinder your work. Entering into shares and investing in various matters is not good at this time, so you should not invest in anything.

Within the family, you should pay close attention to the health of your family members. And be careful of scammers. As for relatives, you should reject invitations to hang out.

In terms of love, even though the situation seems normal, be careful of going out to find temporary happiness. You will suffer from illness and bring disaster into your home.

For health, be careful of illness and accidents during this period. Therefore, you should not travel far during this period. Be sure to have a health check-up and exercise.

Support Days: 3 Nov., 7 Nov., 11 Nov., 15 Nov., 19 Nov., 23 Nov., 27 Nov.
Lucky Days: 4 Nov., 16 Nov., 28 Nov.
Misfortune Days: 9 Nov., 21 Nov.
Bad Days: 10 Nov., 12 Nov., 22 Nov., 24 Nov.

Month 11 in the Snake Year (7 Dec 25 - 5 Jan 25)

This month, the horoscope of those born in the year of the Rat is in the area of energy obstruction, which will cause both good and bad things to appear alternately. You should be careful of unexpected expenses that will cause your cash flow to lack liquidity. What you should do during this time is to plan and manage your finances and accounts well. Do not do activities that are too big for you. If you cannot turn it over fast enough, you will get hurt and lose your reputation.

In terms of work, you should often meet and talk with those you have to do transactions with to strengthen good relationships. When signing contracts, be careful of subordinates making mistakes or causing damage.

This month, your direct income is still good, but you should play with money from your windfall in moderation. Do not spend too much, or you will not get hurt. Avoid investing in illegal businesses, including counterfeit goods or tax evasion. Be careful of lawsuits and being caught in the crossfire and being held criminally liable for things you did not do. During this period, you should closely monitor and collect debts. Be careful of bad debts.

There are often disagreements within your family during this period. You may need to reduce your stubbornness and talk things out to reach an understanding. Try not to let a small issue escalate into a big one that cannot be fixed.

In terms of health, during this period, be careful of accidents both while working and traveling.

In terms of love, don't be indifferent. You still have to keep approaching each other to find success. And you have to keep giving time to take care of each other a lot. Avoid sarcastic words and gestures. This will bring back the good atmosphere.

Support Days: 1 Dec., 5 Dec., 9 Dec., 13 Dec., 17 Dec., 21 Dec., 25 Dec., 29 Dec.

Lucky Days: 10 Dec., 22 Dec.
Misfortune Days: 3 Dec., 15 Dec., 27 Dec.
Bad Days: 1 Dec., 6 Dec., 16 Dec., 18 Dec., 28 Dec., 30 Dec.

Amulet for The Year of the Rat
"Bodhisattva Pu Xian riding an elephant"

Those born in the year of the Rat this year should set up and worship the sacred object "Phra Bodhisattva Phuxian riding an elephant" to enhance their fortune. Place it on your work desk or cash desk to ask for his power and authority to help grant happiness, fortune, and good luck, and help dissolve disasters and turn bad events into good ones, promote careers and businesses to progress and flourish, and bring in an abundance of money.

In a chapter on advanced Feng Shui, it is mentioned that the deities who will descend to reside in the Mie Keng (house of destiny) of the year are deities who can bring both good and bad fortune to the person of that year's destiny. Therefore, worshiping to enhance your fortune with the deities who descend to reside in your birth year is considered to have the best results and have the greatest impact on you. This is to rely on the power of that deity to help protect you while your destiny is declining and having bad karma to alleviate it. At the same time, ask for his blessing to help your business and trade run smoothly as desired, and bring glory and prosperity to you and your family.

Those born in the year of the Rat or Mie Keng (horoscope house) in the zodiac sign Zhi, this year there will be obstacles along the way that you have to jump over and there will be frequent conflicts with others. It is recommended that you use both soft and hard strategies when facing difficult situations because the planets that orbit your zodiac sign this year are the "virtue and moon" planets, which will help you escape from hardships, experience prosperity, and gain honor and fame. The "happiness and fortune" planets will help those who work regularly to have outstanding and recognized work. This year is considered another year that you will have good fortune in terms of finances and career prosperity. There will be people who will help and support you. However, in your horoscope bad stars are orbiting to spread their influence, namely the "Tiang Ae" planet (misfortune), which affects the safety of your family members. Be careful of health problems and accidents, the "Chi Sick" planet (backstabbing planet), and the lawsuit planet, which will cause fights for your career, and arguments with others. Be careful of disputes with coworkers and lawsuits.

In addition, you must be careful of accidents both inside and outside the house. At night, when traveling, you must be careful for your own safety. In terms of love, you will find an interesting lover this year. But let me tell you one thing: don't be indecisive. Health is uncertain. There is a possibility of problems with your mouth and teeth. Therefore, if you want to solve the problem and eliminate the bad stars and support the good stars to be even stronger, you should set up and worship "Phra Bodhisattva Phuxian riding an elephant" to ask for his power and authority to protect you from danger, promote your business and business to progress and flourish, increase your wealth, and have the opportunity to be promoted to another level. "Phra Bodhisattva Phuxian riding an elephant" or as the Chinese and Thai-

Chinese people know him as "Pho Eang Pho Sak" or "Phu Xian Pho Sak", some call him "Phra Samattabhadra Maha Bodhisattva riding an elephant". He is known as a Bodhisattva who excels in conduct and great perseverance. He has a great determination to save the world from suffering without fear of hardship. The image of his elephant-ridden Buddha is "White Elephant with Six Tusks" because "elephants" are considered animals that are resilient and enduring. It is a metaphor for saving all living beings from all suffering, which is a task that requires great patience and sacrifice to overcome the desires and lusts of all living beings.

In the temple's main hall, "Phu Xian Bodhisattva" will be on the right, serving the Lord Buddha Sakyamuni. "Phu Xian Bodhisattva riding a lion" will be on the left. Those who worship and pay homage to Phu Xian Bodhisattva usually ask for his blessings to grant them success in various aspects, whether it be in their careers or their businesses, and their wishes are often fulfilled.

From the appearance of Phu Xian Bodhisattva, his left hand will hold a Yu Yi jade staff to grant power, honor, and followers to those born in the year of the Rat, so that only happiness and peace and happiness will come to them and their families.

In addition, those born in the year of the Rat should wear a lucky pendant in the shape of "Phu Xian Bodhisattva on an elephant" around their necks or carry it with them when traveling near or far from home, so that they person will be filled with auspicious treasures, have prosperity and progress in both business and trade, and have a peaceful and happy family throughout the year, resulting in better and faster efficiency and effectiveness than before.

Good Direction: Southeast, North, and Southwest
Bad Direction: South
Lucky Colors: Blue, Gray, Blue, White, Gold, and Silver

Lucky Times: 07.00 – 08.59, 15.00 – 16.59, 23.00 – 02.59.
Bad Times: 11.00 – 11.59, 13.00 – 14.59, 17.00 – 18.59.

Good

Luck

For

2025